WATCH YOUR ALTITUDE!

by Lisa Moore
illustrated by Rob Kneebone

Harcourt
SCHOOL PUBLISHERS

Cover, ©PhotoDisc/Punch Stock; p.4, ©Ingram Publishing SuperStock; p.10, ©David Young-Wolff/PhotoEdit; p.12, ©Galen Rowell/CORBIS; p.15, ©David Samuel Robbins/CORBIS.

Printed in China

ISBN 10:   0-15-380477-7
ISBN 13:   978-0-15-380477-9

Ordering Options
ISBN 10:   0-15-377149-6 (Grade 5 Collection)
ISBN 13:   978-0-15-377149-1 (Grade 5 Collection)
ISBN 10:   0-15-380687-7 (package of 5)
ISBN 13:   978-0-15-380687-2 (package of 5)

2 3 4 5 6 7 8 9 10 0940 17 16 15 14 13 12 11 10 09

One Hiker's Tale

Alice had planned her trip to Arizona weeks in advance. She'd leave her home in Los Angeles, California, elevation 275 feet (84 m), on a Tuesday morning and make the seven-hour drive in one day. That would get her to her sister Sarah's home in Flagstaff, Arizona, elevation 6,500 feet (1,981 m) by dinner. On Wednesday, Sarah would show Alice around Flagstaff. Then they would get their gear secured on top of the car for a long weekend of hiking and climbing in the nearby Coconino National Forest. "You'll want plenty of time to get accustomed to the altitude before we do any climbing," Sarah said.

On Monday morning, Alice's car broke down, not far from her apartment. She had it towed to her regular mechanic, and, after a certain amount of begging, he promised to have it fixed by late Tuesday afternoon. Alice figured she could drive straight through Tuesday night and sleep late in Flagstaff on Wednesday. She called Sarah to tell her about the change in plans.

The car wasn't ready until Thursday afternoon! Alice picked it up at 4:00 P.M. and headed east. She arrived exhausted at her sister's just before midnight. Over a late night snack, Sarah suggested that they drop their plan to climb Humphreys Peak, but Alice was determined. She'd been looking forward to this for weeks.

"Don't worry," Alice said. "I'm in great shape. I've been jogging three or four days a week and doing yoga classes. Also, don't forget, I'm ten years younger than you!"

"If only you'd let me forget," laughed Sarah.

On Friday, one thing led to another, so by the time Alice and Sarah arrived at the base of the Weatherford Trail, elevation 8,024 feet (2,446 m), it was 4:30 P.M. They decided to hike just two to three miles (2.3–4.8 km) and make camp for the night. The going was fairly easy, and the trail, winding up through aspens and huge ponderosa pines, was breathtaking.

Halfway up, Alice's breath started coming short. Three quarters of the way up, she was feeling light-headed and giggling uncontrollably. Finally, at about 7:30 P.M., she stumbled into the campsite and had a minor collision with a ponderosa pine.

"You chill out, honey, and drink plenty of water," said Sarah. "I'll set the tent up and get a fire going for dinner."

From Los Angeles, Alice had gained 9,000 feet (2,743 m) in elevation in under thirty hours. After dinner, she crawled into the tent exhausted, but she woke up several times during the night. She laid there, heart pounding, trying unsuccessfully to focus her thoughts and get some sleep.

In the morning, Alice felt fine. That's what she told herself (and Sarah) anyway. After a good breakfast, they set off. They thought they could easily reach the Humphreys Peak summit, elevation 12,633 feet (3,851 m) by 4:00 P.M. Then they'd descend a short ways and camp. On Sunday, they'd finish the descent and drive back to Flagstaff.

However, by noon, Alice was gulping for air. When she wasn't gulping, she was yawning. They stopped for lunch. Alice wasn't hungry, but her breathing had settled down. Shortly after they'd set out once again, the headache hit. Alice carried medicine to relieve all kinds of aches and pains. She took two pills, and the headache went from splitting to nagging. She tried to ignore it. "We're so close to the top!" she thought. "I just know I can make it."

By the time she and Sarah reached 12,000 feet (3,658 m), though, Alice's head was pounding. She was stumbling over every bump in the trail. Then she started vomiting. "Help," she said weakly.

Sarah put her arm around Alice. "Honey," she said, "we're done. We're going down now."

With Sarah's help, Alice more or less slid down the trail. They reached a dirt road at about 9,600 feet (2,926 m), and Sarah used her cell phone to call the park service. A ranger kindly delivered them to their car at the base of the trail.

Back at Sarah's home in Flagstaff, Alice managed to get herself in and out of the shower and into bed. The next morning, she felt better——still a little weak and nauseated, but better.

"I guess I should have paid more attention to what was happening to me," admitted Alice.

Early in the first century A.D., about 2,000 years ago, a Chinese general wrote in a report to Emperor Wudi of the Han Dynasty, "South of Mount Pishan . . . travelers have to climb over Mount Greater Headache, Mount Lesser Headache, and The Fever Hill, where they will develop a fever, turn pallid, feel a headache, and vomit. . . ."

Acute Mountain Sickness

What happened to Alice and why did it happen? Traveling from Los Angeles to Flagstaff, Alice gained over 6,000 feet (1,829 m) of elevation in about eight hours. Hiking during the next two days, she gained another 6,000 feet (1,829 m).

On the first day of climbing, she experienced shortness of breath. She felt light-headed and silly. By the time she reached camp, she was staggering and exhausted. That night, she slept poorly. She had a racing heartbeat and felt unfocused and confused. The following morning she felt better, but then, as she climbed higher, she got a pounding headache. Nausea set in, and she began vomiting.

You have Acute Mountain Sickness if you've climbed 8,000 feet (2,438 m) or more and you have a headache in combination with one or more of the following symptoms:

- Loss of appetite, nausea, and vomiting
- Fatigue or weakness
- Dizziness or light-headedness
- Difficulty sleeping
- Confusion
- Staggering gait

In fact, Alice had what doctors call Acute Mountain Sickness (AMS). Alice thought that because she was young and fit, she could handle the change in altitude. She was wrong. Anyone can get AMS. Some people adjust more quickly than others to the thin air at high altitudes; but it is still essential for everyone to follow the rules of altitude sickness prevention.

In 1590, in Peru, a Spanish priest named José de Acosta wrote this of his journey across the Andes Mountains: "When I came to . . . the top of this mountain, I was suddenly surprised with so mortal a pang, that I was ready to fall . . . to the ground . . . [I]f this had continued, I should undoubtedly have died."

Too High, Too Fast

The secret to preventing altitude sickness is not a secret at all: give yourself plenty of time to adjust to the conditions at high altitudes. Stamina and strong, flexible muscles will help you make a steep, rugged climb. The right clothing will help you withstand cold mountain temperatures and strong winds. Only time will allow your body to adjust to lower amounts of oxygen in the air. DON'T CLIMB TOO HIGH TOO FAST!

The first 8,000 feet (2,438 m) of a climb should be spread over at least two days. Three is better. After that, climbing 1,000 feet (305 m) each day is enough. Our friend Alice gained 12,000 feet (3,658 m) of elevation in two and a half days. That's over two miles (3.2 km) straight up! As you make a gradual climb, changes will happen in your body that will help it get the oxygen it needs. You will become acclimated to the thin air.

When you take a breath, your chest gets larger. Inside the chest, the lungs also get larger. Air rushes in to fill tiny air sacs in the lungs called *alveoli*. Fine vessels carry blood past the alveoli. Oxygen from the air in the lungs passes into the blood. It bonds with a substance in the blood called hemoglobin. The oxygen is carried in the blood by the hemoglobin to every part of the body.

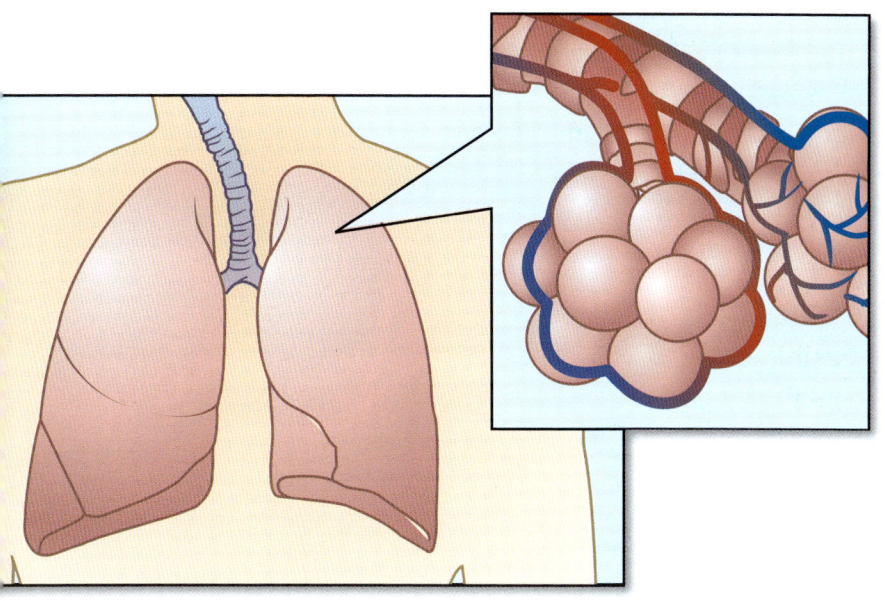

Several things happen as you acclimate, or get used to, to thin air:

1. Your breathing settles to a more rapid pace.
2. Over time, your lungs expand more fully, and you can take in more air with each breath.
3. Your heart pumps steadily at a faster rate. That means that blood moves at a faster rate past the alveoli: there's less oxygen in the air, but the blood picks it up more quickly.
4. Finally, the body actually makes more hemoglobin than usual. That means that the blood can pick up more and more of whatever oxygen is in the air. The body is smart. It will make these changes to assure that it gets the oxygen it needs, but it needs time to do all this.

"It's okay to get AMS—but it's not okay to die from it!" says Peter Hackett, an altitude sickness expert. Hackett—and all of the experts—give us the same simple rule for climbing: *If you have symptoms of mountain sickness, go back down immediately. Never climb any higher. You could get worse, and you might die.*

You remember that one of the symptoms of mountain sickness is confusion. Mountain sickness actually affects your ability to think well. This can get worse with time, and poor thinking can lead to poor decisions, so don't wait around—turn around. Following this rule is the best decision you can make.

Mountain Sickness and the Brain

Until recently, researchers studying mountain sickness focused on the way that oxygen gets into our bodies: the oxygen transport system. Now they are turning their attention to the brain.

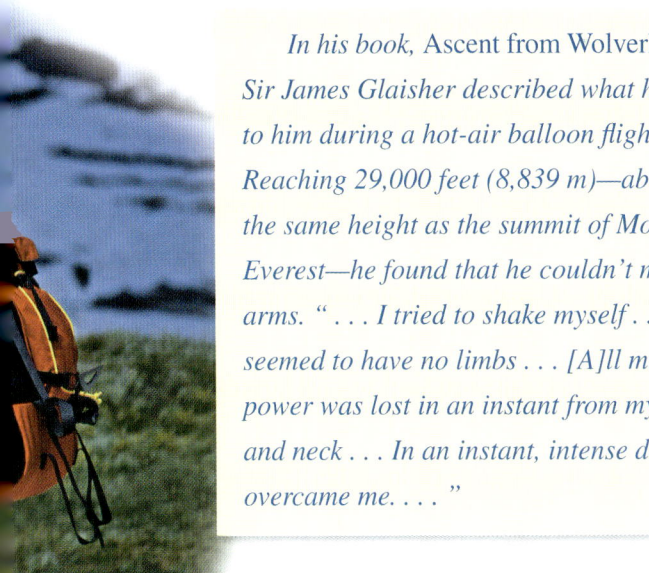

In his book, Ascent from Wolverhampton, *Sir James Glaisher described what happened to him during a hot-air balloon flight. Reaching 29,000 feet (8,839 m)—about the same height as the summit of Mount Everest—he found that he couldn't move his arms. " . . . I tried to shake myself . . . but I seemed to have no limbs . . . [A]ll muscular power was lost in an instant from my back and neck . . . In an instant, intense darkness overcame me. . . . "*

"[I]t's the brain that holds the secrets to mountain sickness," says Peter Hackett. "Brain research is in its infancy. As the secrets of the brain become unlocked over the next twenty-five years, so will the mysteries of mountain sickness and adaptation to high altitude."

What researchers have already discovered is that when a person gets mountain sickness, their brain swells. The heart pumps more blood into the brain, and that causes it to get a bit bigger. The veins and capillaries carrying blood around the brain begin to leak. The fluid that leaks out stays in the brain and causes it to enlarge even more.

Researchers don't know why, but they do know that brain swelling affects how we think. Thinking slows down—and the slower you think, the harder it is to think a problem through. It also becomes harder to remember things, including words. In extreme cases, people suffering from mountain sickness may even have hallucinations, that is, they see things that aren't there.

On the following page are examples of two tests that Peter Hackett and his team give climbers to test how they are thinking at high altitudes. Find a friend and try them out.

Stroop Test

The Stroop Test addresses mental flexibility. Say out loud the color of the letters in each word, not the color the word says. Don't be surprised if it turns out to be harder than it looks!

RED GREEN BLUE BROWN RED GREEN
BLUE BROWN RED GREEN BLUE BROWN
RED GREEN BLUE BROWN

Remembering Sentences

Do this test with a friend. One of you will read each sentence, and the other will try to repeat it exactly. The reader should time the repeater and count the errors. This tests how well you concentrate and remember.

1. Please read pages 20 through 43 and then, based on what you read, answer all seven questions on page 44.
2. The sky was as clear as a blank page of paper interrupted only by a V of Canada geese flying south for the winter.
3. Our flight arrived at the airport an hour late, so we missed our connecting flight to Cleveland and missed Vinnie's wedding.

Time elapsed before response	Time taken to respond	Errors

Getting Extreme

Climbing to extreme altitudes, above 17,000 feet (5,182 m), is serious business. Only expert climbers can scale peaks like Mount Everest. The health hazards include frostbite, sunburn, and any injury that could result from a fall. At those altitudes, to preserve energy, the body streamlines its functions: wounds do not heal, and the stomach does not digest food. Climbers need to be aware of these hazards to avoid them.

For extreme climbers, the hazard at the top of the list is mountain sickness. Climbers must ascend in careful stages in order to safely build acclimation levels. Climbing Everest, for example, takes seven to eight weeks, but only about three weeks are spent climbing. Between short climbs, there's a lot of time for rest and acclimation.

Chances are, you won't be climbing Everest any time soon. However, you may plan a weekend climb to a local peak or ski at a high altitude resort. Be smart. Tell your companions what you've learned about altitude sickness. DON'T CLIMB TOO HIGH TOO FAST! Also, never be ashamed to ask for help if and when you need it.

Think Critically

1. Explain why it is true that altitude sickness is more about the brain than about the lungs.

2. Consider this opinion from page 10: *The body is smart.* What are three facts in this book that support it?

3. What is your opinion of the anecdote the writer included on pages 3-8 called "One Hiker's Tale"? Did this story help your understanding of the subject matter? If so, how? If not, why not?

4. What did you like best about this book?

5. Name three ways in which AMS is like the flu. Name three ways in which it is different.

 **Science**

Make a High Altitude Safety Poster Use some of the information from this book to make a poster about climbing safety for your school library or science classroom. Write a title that asks a question, and then answer that question with a combination of diagrams, charts, text, and pictures. Hang your poster somewhere where others can see it and learn from it.

School-Home Connection Share with family members some of the things you learned in this book. Then talk about why you think people risk their health to do things like mountain climbing and other extreme sports.

Word Count: 2,114